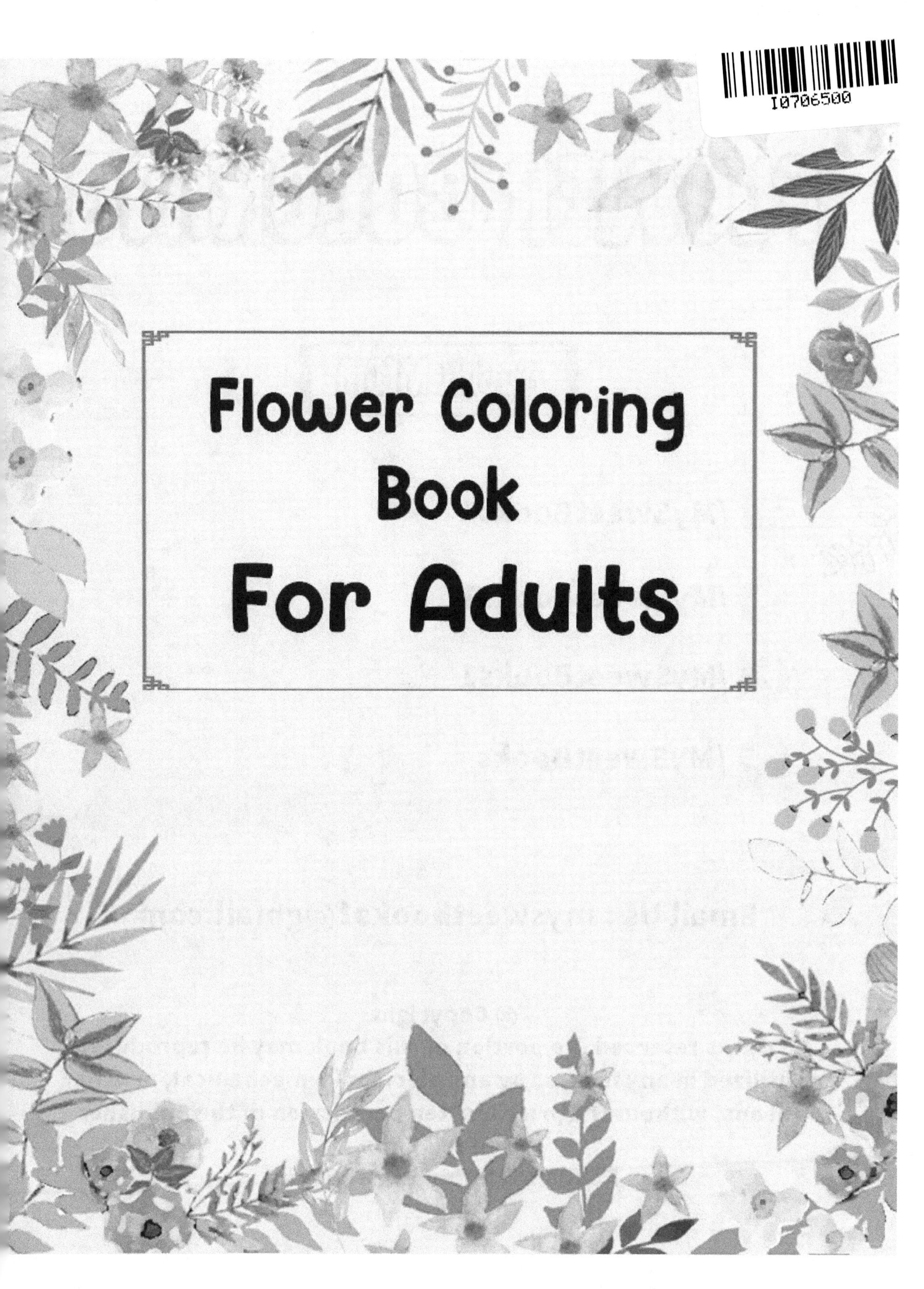

Flower Coloring Book
For Adults

FLOWER COLORING

SOCIAL MEDIA

f /MySweetBooks1

t /MySweetBooks1

i /MySweetBooks1

p /MySweetBooks

Email Us : mysweetbooks1@gmail.com

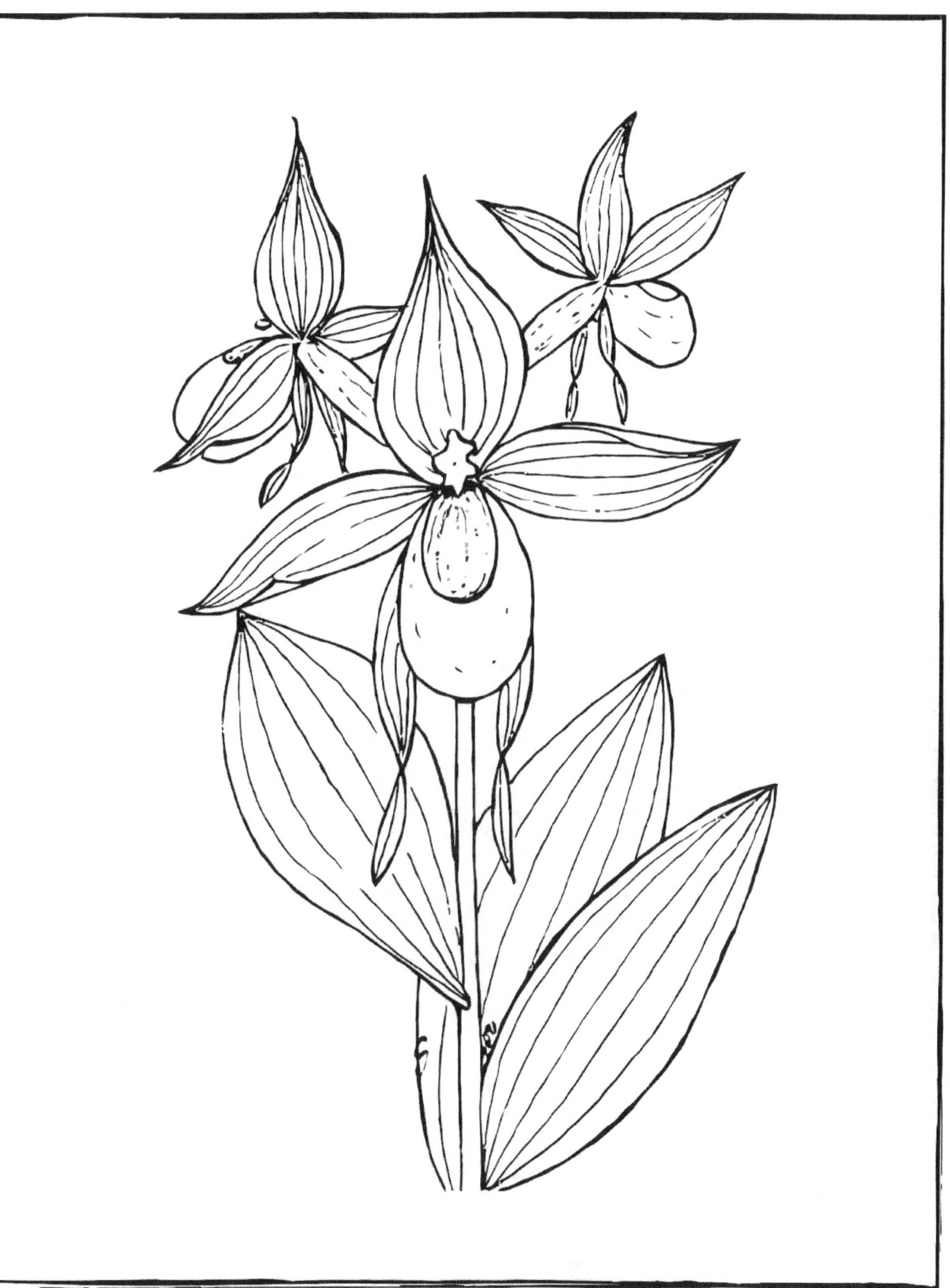

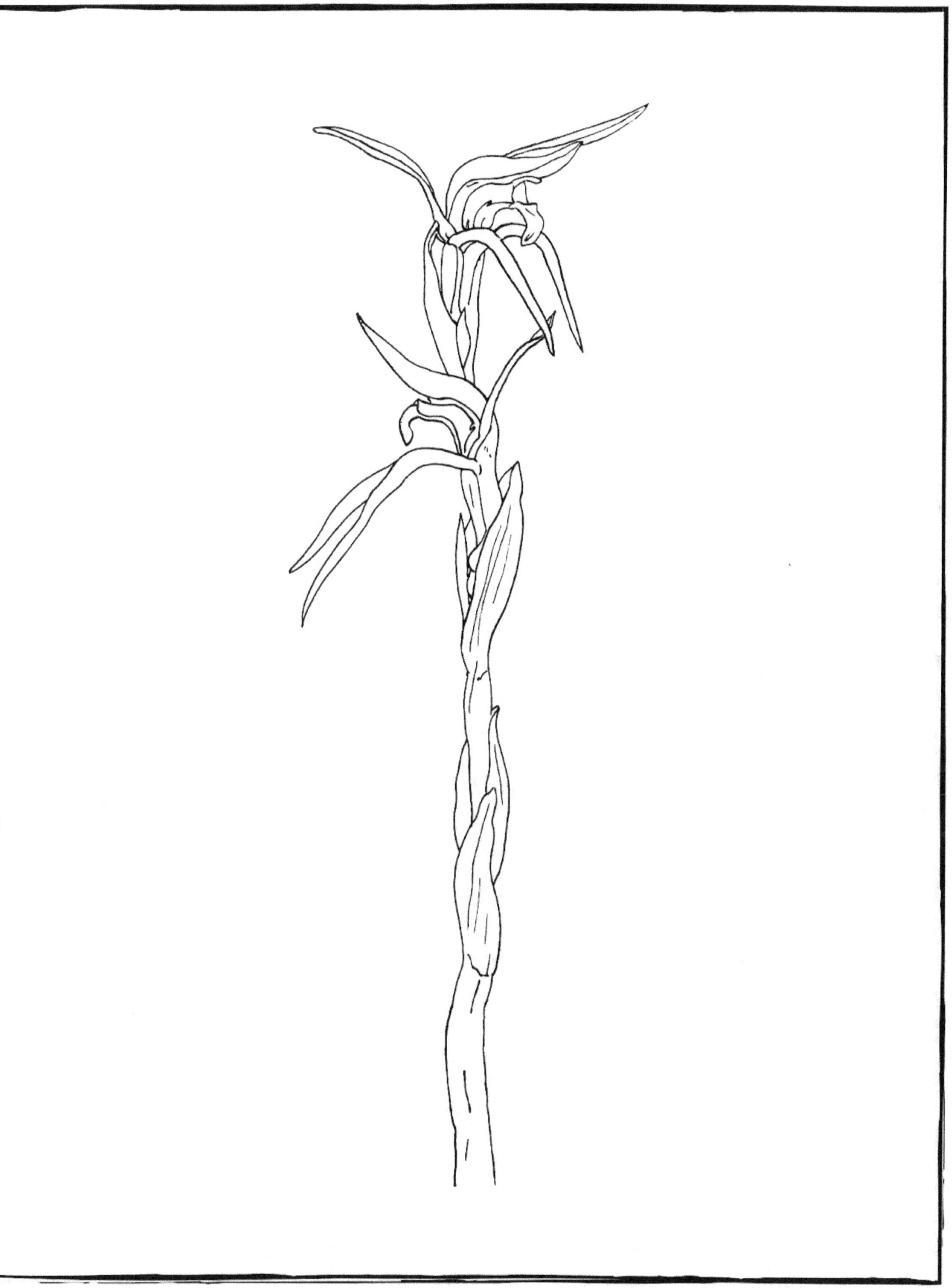

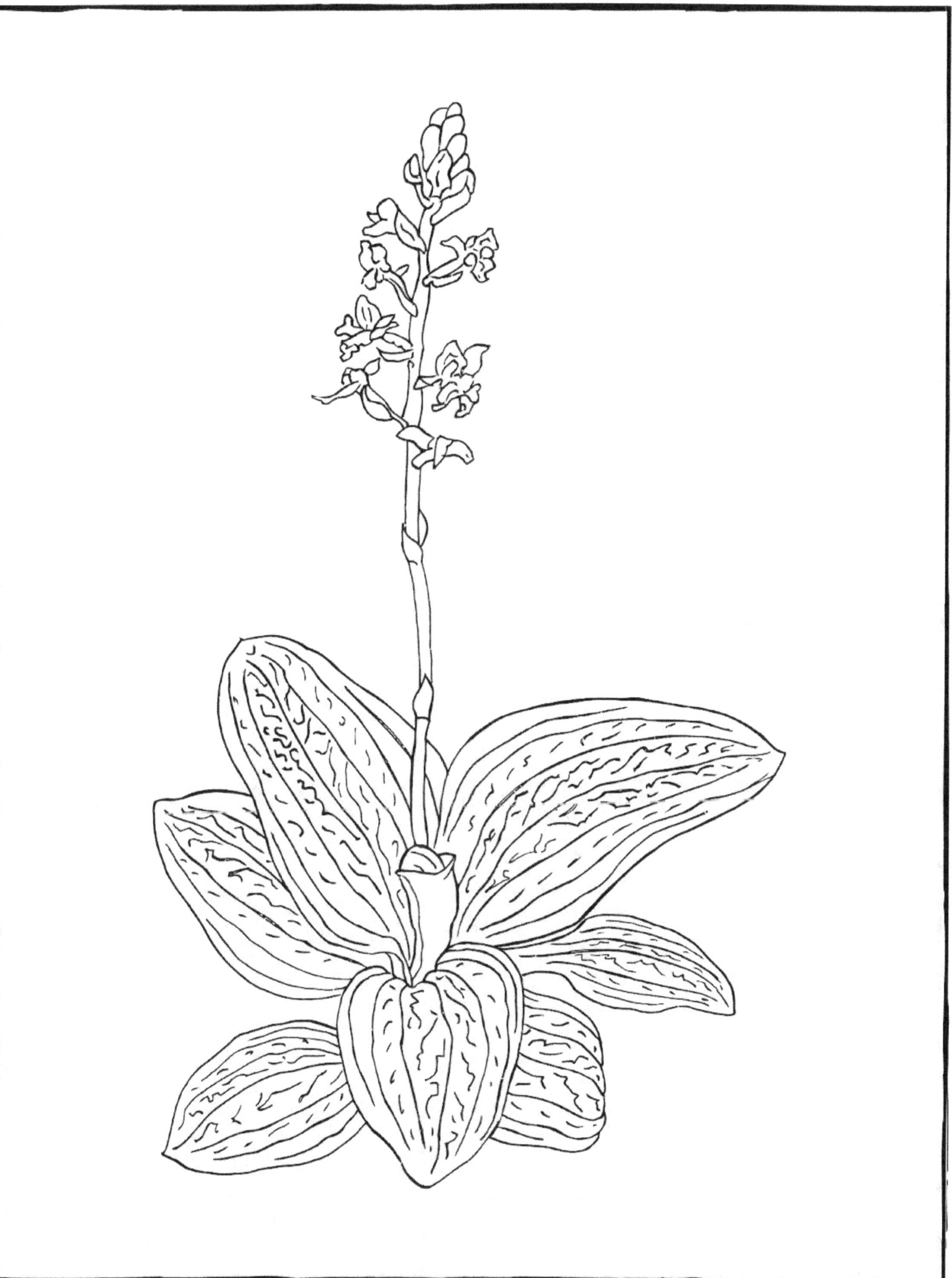

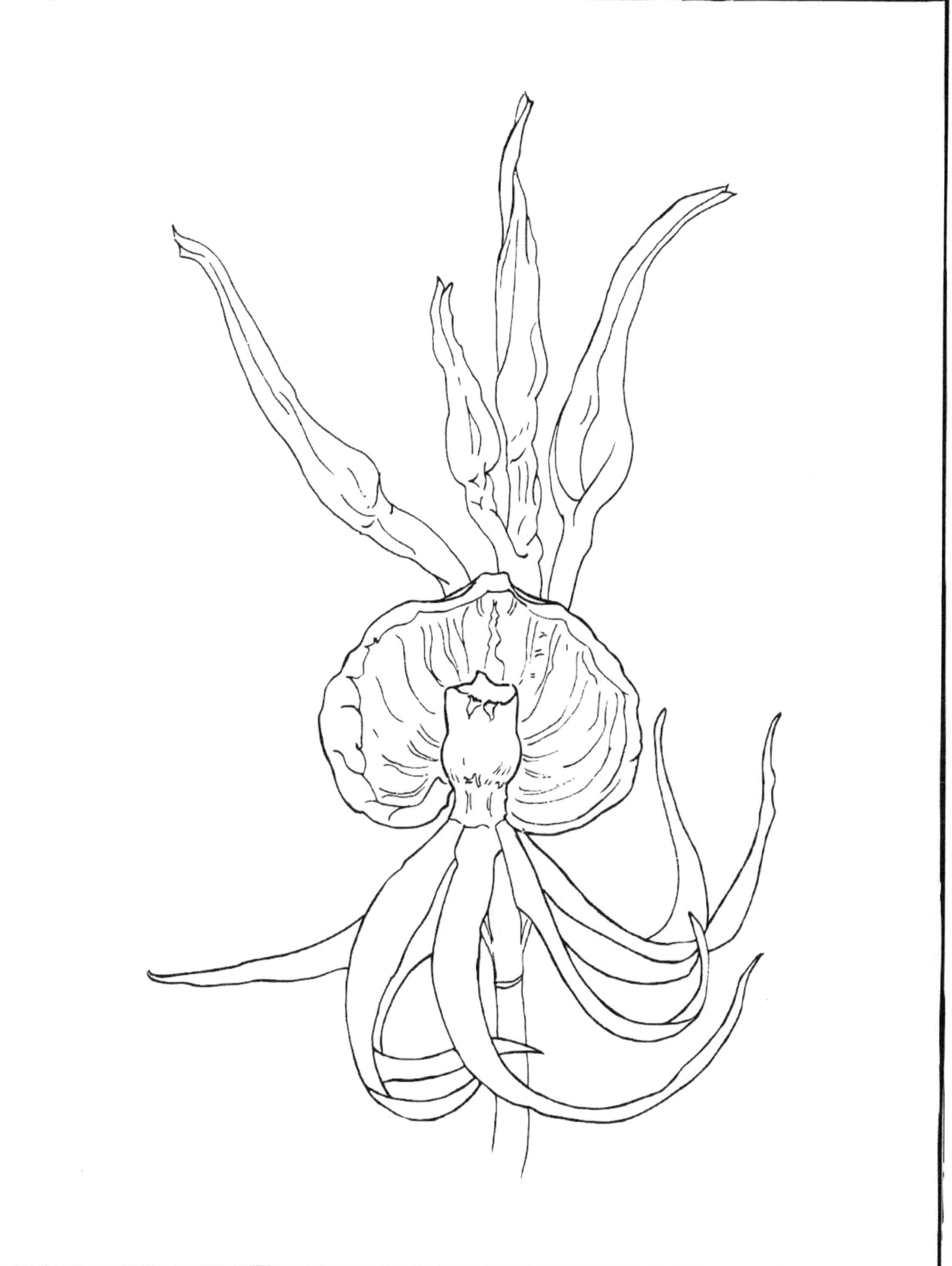

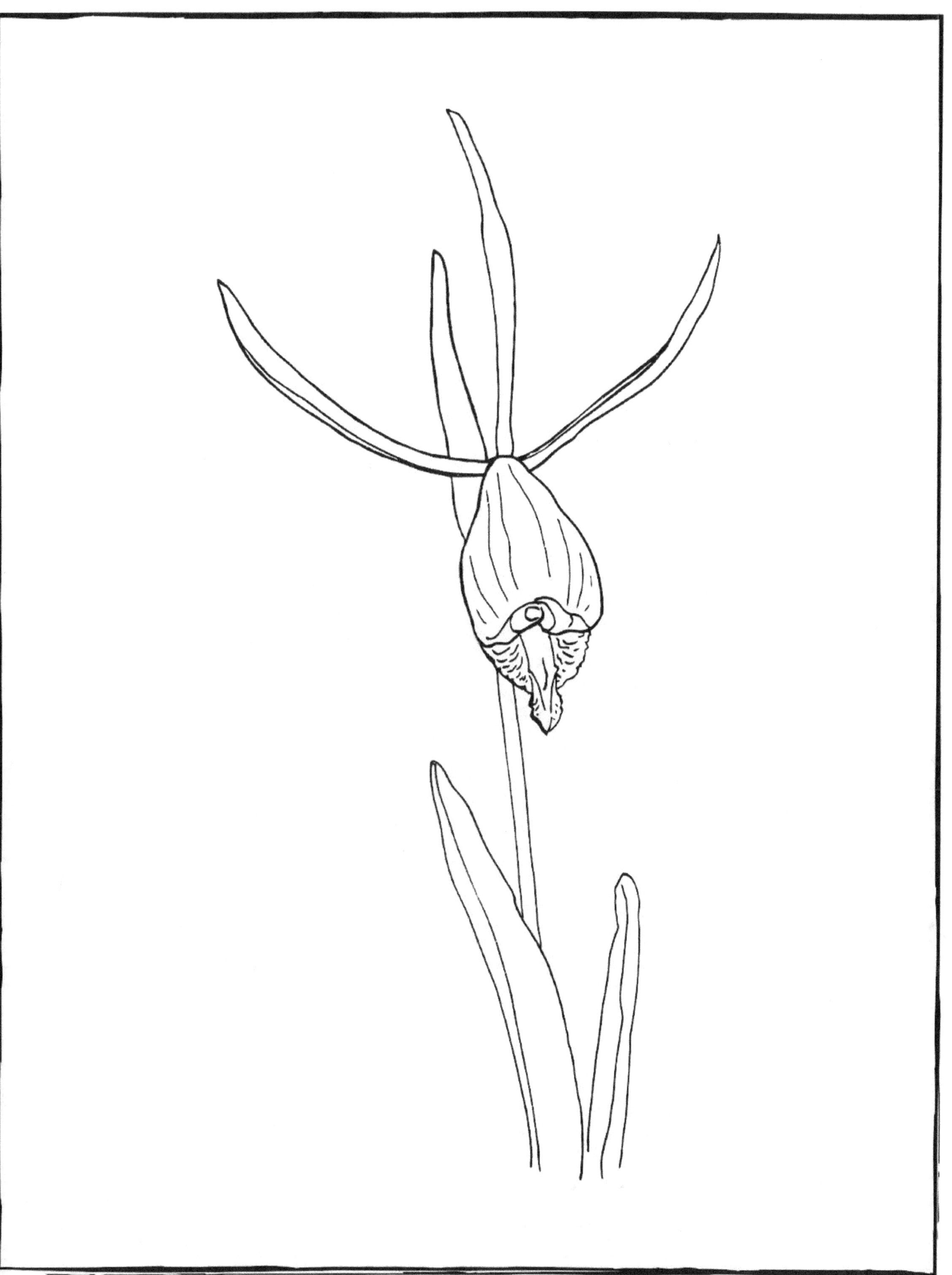

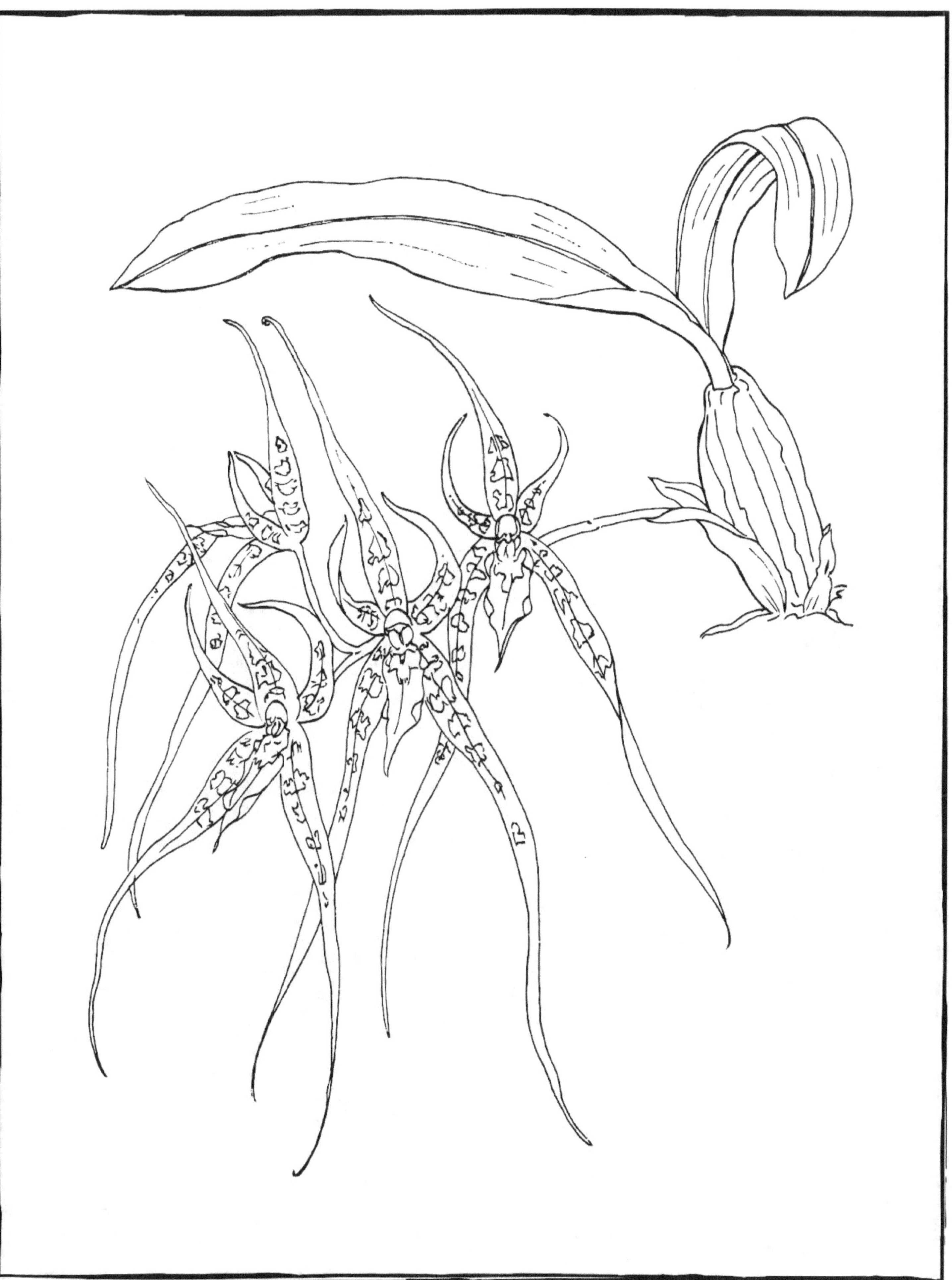

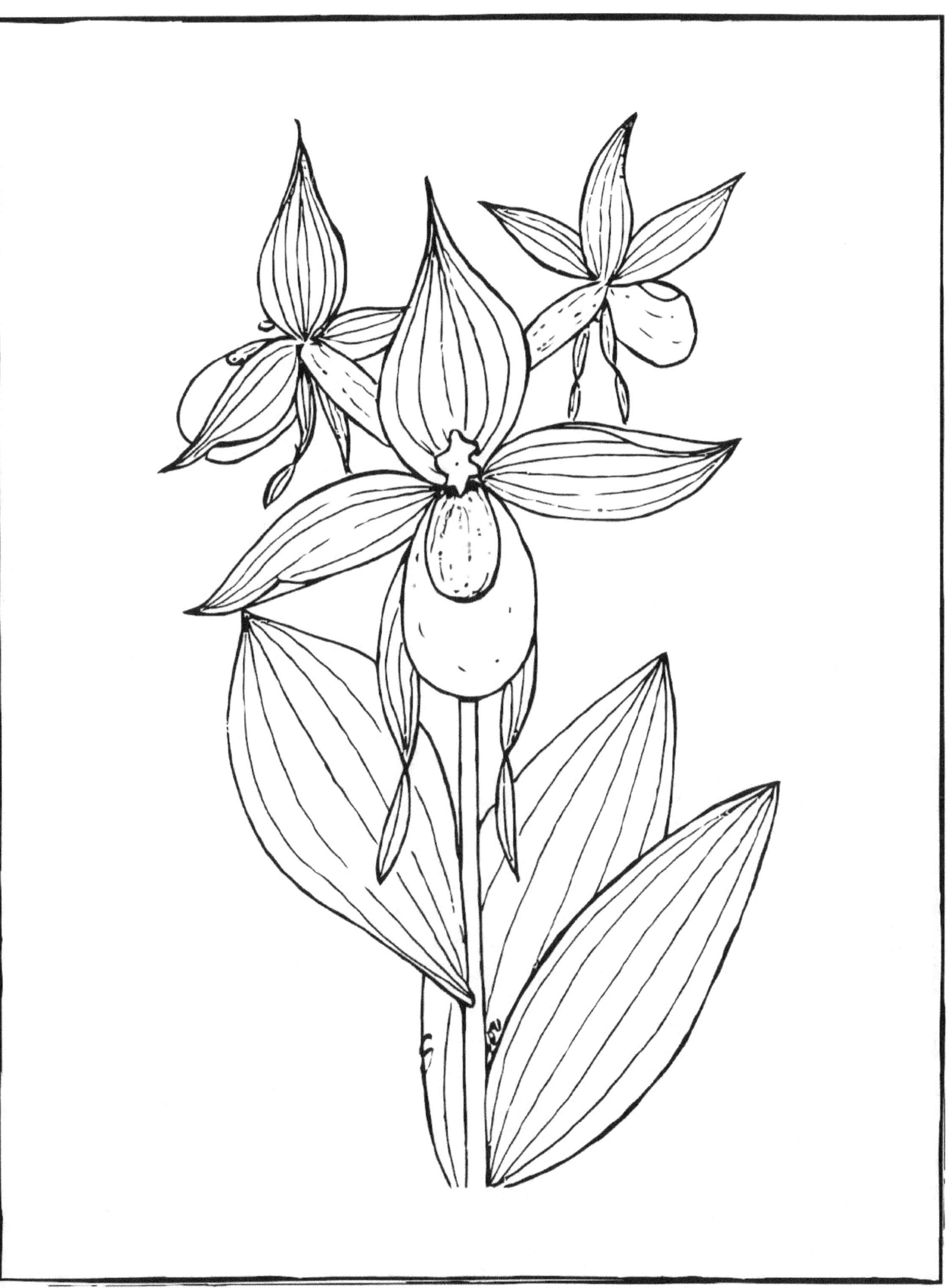